SHINE HIGH

UPLIFTING REFLECTIONS AND MOTIVATIONAL POETRY FOR DAILY INSPIRATION

NORDI HIKARI

Shine High

ISBN: 978-1-0689185-1-3

Dedicated to my Divine Mother of the Universe, who inspired me to pursue my dreams.

Create **Your** Divine Legacy On Your **Own** Terms.

NORDI HIKARI

You can't just sit there and wait for people to give you that golden dream. You've got to get out there and make it happen for yourself.

DIANA ROSS

Knowing is not enough, we must apply. Willing is not enough, we must do.

BRUCE LEE

CHAPTER 1
RED ASCENSION

I am the Storm,
The Warrior of Light.
I AM the Storm,
The Dragonfly of the Night.

IN MOTHER GOD SHE TRUSTS

Gracefully she walks,
Powerfully she talks,
Happily she works,
Magically she loves,
For she inspires all genders,
Letting God be her defender!

In Mother God she trusts.

MADE IN M.E.

Made in Mother Earth,
Funded by God,
I trust my self-worth.

THE ANCIENT ROOT

Born by a set of stars,
My soul shoots outward so far.
Like the cosmos expanding indefinitely,
I manifest thought energy.

As light speeds toward my heart's desire,
I root myself in positivity,
And awake my inner fire!

SPIRITUALIZE ONESELF

The universe guides us all.
We all must trust.
As spirit calls,
To find balance is a must!

CHANGING WINDS

Surfing along the threads of grindstones,
Impressions of thoughts uplift my being
As I paint a new world
And explore the depths of higher poetry.

IT'S YOUR TURN

Do not stop.
Do not settle.
Do not give up; Soar
to a higher level; RISE
to the TOP!

MARK THY FATE

Have no fear.
The Divine is here.
Step into your glory.

Your fate shall be clear.

STEP INTO LOVE

Finding happiness can be yours.
Step with God,
And believe
That everything you've planted can be yours!

A GIRL CALLED LOVE

I knew a girl called Love.
She saw the beauty in everything,
Loved sharing her heart,
and giggling at every wonderful thing.

Worry was but a fragment of her big imagination
'Cause she adored singing every morning,
Shrinking every particle of fear, setting them adrift on the
wind,
Just loving the fun of running and watching the butterflies
fly
nearby. With her chin raised up high

She mastered the art of daydreaming and figuring out her
whys,
Slowly transforming her visions into mellow meditations.
Her soulful liberation against the wind
her way of rebelling,
Of giving herself a voice!
She wanted her very OWN,
Her own life,
Her own story.

Like her mommy always said, "A woman has to have her
OWN."
HER OWN.

No woman is an island.
No woman stands alone.

But down in the country,
Her new passion was hers.
Owning her own was ever so clear,
And it was controlling her own destiny
And watching her beloved multiply heavenly
While loving experiences amassed from her giving,
That made her destiny golden.

And she knew this.

She has her mother's spirit,
A drive most people couldn't comprehend.
And when she came to accept her calling,
And no one would lend a hand to her plans,
That didn't stop her.
She had the secret weapon:

Her power!
Her power of speech,
Power of words,
Power of thought,
Power of sharing.

This is who I am.

ME!

This is a man's world, but I still enjoy the love of me
As an extension of mama's legacy.

I do things easily.
In repentance, I live free.
I am the "B" of Bees
THE QUEEN BEE.
With buzzing humming internally,
Healing waves of peace rain down on thee!

But this girl of excitement
had brief third-sight eruptions.
Indulging in night's pleasures had
at times fogged her eyesight.
For that girl called Love battled tyrants early on
But now she's full of more strength to finally do what she
says.
Now that she's done the work,
Her ship is coming ashore.
She is fully awake;
The dawn is hers!
And yes!

A work of progress
Is birthed from the fire!
Blessed by God's blessings,
Emerging from inside out,
A blazing force with desires,
A passionate individual rises without a doubt!
She is love.
For she raises the vibrations of the earth,
Again knowing her worth.
For this girl called Love,
This girl who received nothing but unconditional love,
Knows it's ALL ABOUT GIVING YOUR ALL,
GIVING YOUR ALL WITH LOVE!

FLOWERFLY ILLUMINED

God made a bed for us to lay
On. We can rest or raise
ourselves up to the highest one.
Since twinkles are easy to come by,
Let the flower-fly of life color
your world to illuminate the sky.

GET MOVING

You can do it if you try.
You can rise.
You can overcome.
When faced with life's challenges, know
That God is on your side.
So trust always
The Divine Presence within.
As you take deep breaths,
Watch your transformation begin.

TRUST IN GOD

Look up to the sunrise
And find your peace.
Be the well that fuels your passion.
Put your trust in a burning leaf
And release.

FOREVER PERSEVERE

No matter how hard the road becomes,
Never give up.
When you have no one to lean on,
Keep looking up.
When the sky turns foggy and dark,
Keep looking up.
When it rains and you can't find your way,
Rise up and set a new path for today.

TAP YOUR HEELS

If you feel alone
When the voyage becomes cold
And there's nothing left to hold,
Start dreaming!
When the world's weight is overwhelming,
When you feel your efforts have been for nothing,
Keep believing!
For in every way, and every day,
better times are coming!

50S CHANNEL

The universe speaks
On a magically touched channel.
It asks for your patience,
So calmly excel
And know all is well.

NAYS TO YEAS

No more sorrow,
No more shame,
No more fear,
No more pain,
For God is near!
Oh yea!

No more sadness,
No more stress,
No more tiredness,
No more worry,
For God's power is within us,
Oh yea!

No more rushing,
No more fighting,
No more suffering,
No more lying,
For God watches over us!
Oh yea!

And,
No more anger,
No more doubt,
No more temptation,
No more without,
For the spirit of God overflows our lives with divine glory!

DO YOU SEE?

Do you see the ever-shining light?
Do you see how special you are?
Do you know that you hold the key to reaching any height?
Do you know how you've made it this far?
Do you see all possibilities as they appear so clear?
Do you know all your hard work will pay off,
And the light at the end of the road is near?

Do you see that you're brave?
Do you know the doors will open all the way if you pray?
And do you see the lovely being that your angels can see?
Do you see how your life is meant to be?
Can you see?
Can you conceive beyond a trillion galaxies?
Can you imaginatively let it be?

HONOR SELF

Honor your light,
Honor your soul,
For it shines divinely bright.
Have faith in your brilliance,
Have faith in your ideas,
For your uniqueness deserves its existence.

CHAPTER 2
ORANGE BURSTS

Happy vibes
Bring
Happy times.

CREATOR

Born of mother nature's womb,
I bloom like a flower
Caressed by summer bees.
I beautifully express cosmic colors of love.

MAMA GOD

Mama God believes in me.
Oh, she loves me.

She comforts all living things.

Working mystically, she watches
over me. Waving
her wand, she works tirelessly,
Raining abundant ideas infinitely.

THE DRAGON FLIES

Imagine living an adventure-filled life
In a fruitful basket ship,
Anchoring your conscious energy to the sky,
Where a heavenly presence purifies your mind.

LET IT PASS

Paddle against the currents.
Do NOT give in to the tidal waves.
Let the storm pass,
And learn to dance in the rain.

BE YOUR BRIGHTEST REFLECTION

Appreciate the sunny side of life.
Be kind to yourself.
Stand tall.
Surround yourself with positive influences.
Enjoy life.
Find the beauty of nature.
Share your joy with strangers.

And live life!

EIGHTH WONDER

Infinitely glowing,
Marching through phases,
No matter what happens,
I will pick up the pieces.
For I will figure it out!
I shall get it done!

WOMAN IN THE MIRROR

A beautiful pearl of the sea
Weeps beneath her veil,
Aspiring for her crown of creative power to prevail.
As it flows out into authentic reality,
She becomes a new woman in the mirror,
Full of faith that her crown will return to the shore,
That the openness of her heart will receive it.

BUBBLING BEING

Grow as an organic soul.
Don't live someone else's dream.
Identify what makes you whole.
Empower a new theme.
For with a focused mind,
You can conquer your walls and achieve your dreams.
It's the perfect time.
YOU.
SHALL.
SEE!

THE TIPPING POINT

Can you wait any longer?
Are you pushing forward?
Is your willpower getting stronger?
Then travel onward; create magic for your journey!
Make your inner magician come alive.
Create your opportunities.
You made it this far!
You will survive!

Letting every action be your center of attention,
Knock down those walls you built!
Your higher mind will erase limitations,
So get on with it!

HIKING DISCOVERY

God does the doing,
But I take the initiative.
Even with the goal in mind,
Auras of thoughts scatter before they align.

But I raise the torch over the water,
Mastering the ways to become smarter,
So I can go with the flow.
And just as so
The wind washes over the hills
Revealing the beauty of creation
I'm gifted with the realization of free will.

Life illuminates with motivation.

MINDFUL CHANGE

As one raises their sacral bubbles of vibrations,
A pool of possibilities appears, amplifying infinitely.
By attuning to one's insight with the power of meditation,
One certainly transforms their outer reality.
Indefinitely.

DO SOMETHING

If you have one hand,
One foot,
Get up and do something!

With even one idea
And a big smile,
You can do something!

With one life
And a big heart,
Spread your wings endlessly.

Doing just one positive thing
Can inspire anything!
So step up,
Go the extra mile,
And Do Your Thing!

BLOOMING THROUGH THE SEASONS

Blooming authentically,
I bloom energetically.
Blooming proudly,
I bloom uniquely.
Blooming purposely,
I bloom into a beautiful being.

EIGHT WAVES

One wave for braveness,
Two waves for confidence,
Three waves for gratefulness,
Four waves for patience,
Five waves for determination,
Six waves for imagination,
Seven waves for divine creation
And eight waves for uplifting motivation!

Embrace the waves with love.

NO X'S

Make no excuses.
You must take a leap of faith.
You have what it takes!
Reach for your dreams,
And don't let your spirit break.
Always be proud of your efforts!
For you are great!

PLAY, PLAY, PLAY

Remember to play
And find joy when you play!
Show up every day,
And go all the way!

RISING STONES

As I create,
I appreciate.
As I appreciate,
I celebrate.
As I celebrate life,
Life expands at a divine rate!

SMILE

Smile

Just smile because your life is worthwhile.
Smile at overcoming your trials.
Smile for the times you were hurt.
Smile even if you're an introvert.

Now smile for you.
Smile and give thanks.
Smile. It's the best thing to do.

Just smile as you move through rough waters.
Smile when no one bothers
Smile brightly for starting over again.
Smile as you face your divine plan.
Smile for every door that has opened.
Smile, for you have been chosen
To compose a life from the words you have spoken.
Smile and STAND TALL.
For the Universal God loves us all!

THE TUNING

I play to the tune of life.
Dwelling in its infinite presence,
I taste the sweet melody of life.
Vibrating with motion,

Thriving on movement,

I let creativity chart the course of my life.

THE MOONLIGHT RAINS

With an orange star above,
Rainbow clouds streak over the night sky,
Shepherding my mind on a full moon,
And showering my heart with love.

YOU CAN MAKE IT

This mission is yours,
So be a magnet of positive light, inhale
your cosmic master plan, exhale
and reclaim your life.
For it's never too late to illuminate
your destiny. Your presence here
Serves a purpose.
Embark on your universal journey,
And own your uniqueness!

CHANGE IS HUMMING

Change is on the horizon,
Only if you have the faith
To make it over the hill,
Where the grass grows taller,
And the sun lays still.
So be driven to move with the wind.
Calmly go within,
And be willing to give in.
For your higher mind is calling.

Just turn the dial to change your frequency.
You have no choice but to renew immediately,
For your divine mind, body, and soul wait patiently!

ASCENDANT

A rising sun materializes sunshine.
It oversees my life.
It governs my mind.
As the mist settles,
I feel nothing but good times.

ONE OF A KIND

Be attracted to the highest frequency,
For positivity prepares the air.
Be excited about your wishes.
Begin your morning with conscious prayer.

So in Oneness, be patient
When manifesting your horn of abundance.
This is yours!
Trust in the process,
And dream more.

WILD WALK

Take a walk on the wild side.
Wiggle your toes in the mud.
Feel your excitement bubbling up inside,
And have some fun!

CHAPTER 3
YELLOW REVIVAL

We are all in this together.
As long as you move forward with faith,
Life will get better.

BE YOUR OWN HERO

I will be my own superhero.
Starting from zero,
I will grow and grow and grow,
Being a golden, positive light and
Saving every soul.

SHE ROARS

Born into infinity,
I manifest
Like the universe, inspiring
a rosy outlook on life.
I compose animated ideas with lioness courage.
For my perception holds infinite wisdom,
Allowing luminous transition,
Transitioning into a luminous state.

HEARTFELT TALK BEGINS

Everything began as a positive.
Everything is a frequency.
Everything begins at the end of a rainbow.
Everything will complete itself in divine order.
Everything is pointing you toward a greater good.
Everything will go according to plan.
Everything teaches you what you need to know.

From your essence will come everything you desire,
And when you enlighten your heart,
All you desire will be yours!

CROSSING THE LINE

Treasure the bottled memories,
Rejoice, and celebrate your victories.
By facing the winds of failure
And battling the tides of Tsushima with laughter,
You'll deserve to wear your crown.
For you are a blazing winner!

DEEP SOULFUL LIVING

Share your happiness in excess.
Wish others the utmost success.
For our lives are better when we wish others well.
So embark on your own tale,
Inspiring others to excel.

WISDOM CHECK

When struck with negativity,
See it as a blessing.
Go in a new direction,
Where greater good awaits,
By reaping the rewards from the lesson.

JUST BECOME

Having money doesn't bring freedom.
Pockets full of coins aren't stepping stones to Queendom,
For freedom prospers from within.
Freedom comes from embracing yourself and
Moving forward so your new life can begin.
Life will bring you both happiness and sadness,
But divine sunlight will return after the cold weather passes.
So let go of your regrets; let go of your fears
To brighten your soul.
Just become present and whole!

I AM JOYFULLY ALIVE

I am joyfully alive to taste the sweetness of honey.
I am joyfully alive to fulfill my life's soul-journey.
I am joyfully alive to see the sun rise.
I am joyfully alive to savor the roses that nature provides.
I am joyfully alive with a depth of gratitude.
I am joyfully alive to evolve a positive attitude.
I am joyfully alive to revive from the warmth of a hug.
I am joyfully alive because of everlasting love!

HUMMINGBIRDS SING

Be the pilot of your own adventure.
Fly as far as you can go.
Drink in the splendor of nature. But
with eyes looking upwards,
Be what you know,

Be the one to uphold your power.
Be the one to make use of every hour!
Just dig deeper for your dreams!
Dig deeply and be a queen!

TAKE A STAND FOR YOUR LIFE

Walk on for the beauty of divine self;
Walk on to extend your health.
Walk on with the strength of a million trees;
Walk on with the energy to breathe.

Walk on like a warrior with a spirit to win;
Walk on even when no one checks in.
Walk on as the wind carries you forward;
Walk on even when you feel tortured.

Walk on with eyes praising the sky;
Walk on expressing a beautiful smile.
Walk on with head held high;
Walk on, for you can survive.

Walk on with a hummingbird heart to inspire;
Walk on with every desire.
Walk on with fire as the ebullient Forrest Gump;
Walk on when you hit a few bumps.

Walk on when the rain pours the hardest;
Walk on like an Egyptian goddess.
Walk on when the sun shines the brightest;
Walk on when the storm gets the wildest.

Walk on when the valley gets steeper and steeper;
Walk on when the ocean gets deeper and deeper.
Walk on like a white dove without wings;
Walk on trusting what the universe brings.

Walk on as a queen would;
Walk on when you're misunderstood.
Walk on till the earth quakes;
Walk on till you wake.

Walk on until you reach your true reality.
Walk on until you tip the scales of gravity!

BE THE ONE

Progress at a good pace,
No need for haste.
Keep pushing yourself,
And be like no one else.
Consistently perform with grace!

HEALING WAVES

Amidst wonders, amongst crumbling ice,
Uncover your eyes
And reach for the skies

By bringing to light your essence.
Fear not ever; fret not ever,
For the tree of knowledge revolves in your presence
So run through the cycle of life
Until you get this assignment right!

SOUL WORDS

God loves you!
God looks after you!
You're never too old
To be bold.
Do what's good for your soul.

SENSE YOUR WORTH

Heighten your power.
Give life to your dreams.
As the rain amplifies the flowers,
Cultivate your self-esteem!

RUMBLE OF THUNDER

Free the rumble in your gut
If you stumble.
But always get back up.
Go!
Be thankful for all occasions.
Go!
Praise your challenges.
See something bigger than yourself.
Grasp your gifts.
And go!

Fly until you can't fly anymore!

BEAUTIFUL ONE

Observe the sunset in a flickering light.
Even when you face challenges,
Be happy from morning to night.
And take that leap of faith into the unknown,
Even if you're standing alone.
Gather the utmost strength on your own!

IF YOU TRY

Be free!
Step into something new.
Breathe!

Find your true purpose;
Cocreate with the universe.
For smiling daily is what your heart deserves.
Once again breathe deeply.
You were born to win!
So walk bravely, my friend,
For your inner child of the universe
Cheers from within!

I KNOW

I Know

I know where I've walked.
I know my burden.
I know my heart.
I know my worth.
So I rise!

Likewise, as I drift into positive currents,
I know the shifts in the wind will push me forward.
My shackles are losing their title.
Once again,
I FEEL LIGHTER!
For I know karma has departed.
Dear butterfly, the universe has responded.

The choice is yours!
YOU know there are options
And yet more options to explore!
Be fearless!
And know you can do this!
But do *I* think I can?

Yes!
I CAN DO THIS!
BY JUST DOING MY BEST!

I know I can give my best and nothing less.
Everything I touch is blessed!
And all good things turn into success! YES!

I know the time is now.
I FEEL IT IN MY BONES!
I know I am loved.
I know I can go up, up, up, and above!
There is always a way,
And another lovely day
Awaits in the sidelines for me to do better.
I know I can smile and be a go-getter,
Facing my gift that reveals my truth.

The work starts only with you.

But did I know I could get up and step up so readily?
Oh, YES!
I know who I am internally.
For the love of Divinity, I was birthed from infinity!
Inspired with the legacies of our great mothers shining on,
I KNOW we need to live fully before it's all gone!

HELLO ...

Time is precious, so don't waste it!
Be your own hero!
Go chase it!
Live out your number one goal today.
The Power is yours!

Don't ever give up on the runway!

SWIRLING LIGHTS OF POWER

Resolutely spring forth over those mountains,
Where you can deeply sow your foundation
With magnetic decrees like,
"Anything is Possible"
And cultivate edicts like,
"Everything is Possible."

But as you give the higher one its power,
Realize your soul is like the seed of a flower.
For your divine legacy is here to stay!
And just like Buddha, you *can* find your way!

CHAPTER 4
GREEN REVIVAL

Adore self,
Cleanse self,
Nurture self,
Strengthen self,
Support yourself,
And love yourself purely.

THE LIVING FORCE

The energy of all life will make a way.
The energy of all life listens to all you say.
The energy of all life loves it when you find your way.
So let love be in your heart, oh, every single day.
Become a lantern of giving
With the goal to live positively.
For it feels oh so good
when you're spiritually winning!

MADE BY LOVE

Be the director of your own film.
Make it with love.
Fill it with flavorful, colorful images,
Letting the storyline flow with the rhythm of life.
Create a masterpiece to inspire humanity to unite.

I CAN UPLIFT MY SOUL

I choose a path of healing.
I choose of life of good living
Forevermore and fully.
I choose to say, "I forgive," in mellow whispers to others.
I choose to preserve my health as I would in divine waters,
Choosing to be a mindful lion in the now.

I choose to unfurl and hereby avow,
I will jump up for joy.
I choose today to enjoy,
Choosing to float on the puffiest of clouds,
Cheering with the heartbeats fluttering around.
I choose loving thee deeply.
I choose to bless all so sweetly,
Choosing to be my own dearest friend.
I choose to love every being till the end.

See,
I choose to be free.
I choose to evolve like a bumblebee.
I choose to live until every daydream is pursued,
Choosing to express a good attitude.

And I choose positive spaces and true love,
Choosing to see the world not from below but from above.
That's why I choose to emit only positive vibes,
Moving on in progressive strides,
Being so thankful for the presence of a mourning dove.
I am forever thankful for my mother's love!

REACH NEW HEIGHTS

Discover your wings.
Find your North Star.
Let your heart sing.
Know who you truly are.

I AM WITH YOU

I will get up;
I will wipe off the dust.
I will be bold;
I will let it out.
I will speak my mind;
I will shake the ground.
I will waste no more time.
I will blow bubbles of big dreams;
I will pop each one
Until each milestone is done.
I will get up again;
I will stay on the right path.
I will see the light at the end of this tunnel;
I will blaze new trails.
I will make happy memories;
I will surround myself with good people.
I will live each day with joy.
I will dance under the stars;
I will listen to my silent disco,
Grooving the night away.
I will stay on course.

For I am on a mission.
I shall rise!
Evolution is mine!
I chose to come back.
I am no longer fighting my predestined path.
I am stronger than the casting of dark shadows.
I am luminous in pure light like a rainbow!

YOURS TRULY

You're at the right place,
Oh, yes!
You're divinely here at the right time,
Oh, yes!
You're eyes are alive with fire,
Oh, yes!

Your inner sense now shines!

RAISE UP YOUR WISH

Open your heart,
And believe it is yours.
When you carry out integral changes,
The universe opens the doors.

ONLY ONE LIFE TO LIVE

With only one life to live,
My reflections are now positive.
For everything has a beginning
From where love flows on endlessly.

GO HIGHER

As unique as a beautiful day,
As unstoppable as ocean waves,
Don't be afraid of your essence.
Appreciate the higher presence!
Your heart loves to shine!

UNBREAKABLE

Being good to myself,
I travel at a steady, sustainable pace.
Taking great care of my health,
I'm chakra-centered in my space.
As I keep on living,
I forgive past mistakes,
Surging above the worrying
For my soul will not break!

NECTAR JUBIE

Each and every day,
I will occupy a space of joyful wonder,
Living a higher life,
Attaining true happiness,
Doing right.

BEYOND POSSIBILITY

I am flush with Divine consciousness,
As a magical being.
I love living with righteousness
And doing inner healing.

As I activate the higher self,
I greet the day with joyful thoughts!
Shooting higher than the stars,
I dream of reaching everything.

Gazing upward,
I
KEEP
ON
BELIEVING!

FIND THE HIDDEN

Be calm in stillness,
So your true self can be found.
Experience peacefulness
While your hands touch the ground.
As your energy unites with your infinite mind
Your purpose will emerge
From where the heart of all knowledge resides!
And there you will find
The real meaning of LOVE

And that's the Divine One Above!

PURE ECSTASY

Your soul is almighty,
So lift up your heart.
The inner child knows only how to be so rejoice and believe.
Forever as energy, and from now till eternity,
Flow with the stream of divine love,
Embrace drops of blessings from above.

JOY TO YOURSELF

Every wish you make,
Every step you take,
All starts with loving you!
For good things do come true
When you achieve that pure harmony
In your heart, in your mind, in your higher self.
You will make it through!

LIFE IS ...

Life is a farm.
Nurture it.
Life is a riddle.
Solve it.
Life is a game.
Win it.
Life is a class.
Master it.
Life is a song.
Sing it.
Life is inspiring.
Feel it.
Life is an experience.
Enjoy it.
Life is a story.
Write it.
Life is a dream.
Believe it.
Life is a goal.
Achieve it.
Life is a struggle.
Learn from it.

Life is a process.

Perfect it.

Life is a ship.

Navigate it.

Life is a joy.

Live it.

Life is a radio station.

Change it.

Life is a lesson.

Learn it.

Life is like a journey.

Embrace it.

Life is an adventure.

Explore it.

Life is a gift.

Cherish it.

Life is a beautiful thing.

Love it!

BECOME

Become a child of light.
Become the hand of Universal love.
Become with all your might.

Become a garden of good vibes.
Become a positive being.
Become the manifestation of a butterfly.

Become the symbol of Maat.
Become a light feather.
Become more than your thoughts!

DIVINE TRUST

Trust in your vibrancy,
And always be yourself.
Life will get easier
When you love thyself.

BE IN LOVE

Be in love with something positive.
Be in love with change.
Be in love with appreciation.

Be in love when the storm comes in with the rain.
Be in love with everything you strive for.

Be in love with human unity.
Be in love with giving more.

Be in love with living your mystical destiny.
Be in love with the cells in and under your skin.

Be in love with divine love.
Be in love with seeking happiness from within.
Be in love with you.

I LOVE THEE

I love thee.
I love all things about me.
I love greeting a new day gratefully.
I love flowing with the wind.
I love arising my true self within.
I've loved me from the beginning,
And as young as I can remember,
I've loved that feeling
Of loving me forever!

WELL-WISHER

My heart rejoices as
essential nature creates
a new world. Pluto
strikes a chord.
Embarking on an odyssey of love with transparency,
I awaken cycles of life energy
To face higher spiritual levels of bliss.

CHAPTER 5
BLUE VIBRATIONS

Gain from any loss.
The coin of life can flip to either side.
You are still the boss.

A SOUL EXPERIENCE

Fly birds fly.
Liberate the sky.
Let thy inner flowers thrive
As I magnify with that most high.

MOTHER MOON SPEAKS

Mother moon is telling me now
To plunge into deep waters
And be proud.

In honor of my loving mother,
I must keep moving.
I have planted the seeds.
Let the universe orchestrate.

WE MUST

It is our duty to always evolve.
With each step I take,
I journey beyond; I travel ever higher.
I take action right now,
For the Creator leads the way!

LISTEN TO THE BREEZE

Listen to the breeze,
Silently awaken,
And the momentum will flow naturally.

TO BE

Be so kind to yourself.
Plant seeds to honor your soul.
Your destiny follows your energy,
So release positivity,
Get moving, and go!

SPRINTING OVER

I will make it over the hurdles.
I will survive what comes my way.
And landing on my feet again,
I will listen to my true calling today!

AN AZURE SHINE

Today is the day to ride with the waves!
Today will be an energetic day.
Today, I am freshly excited about my future.
Today, I will have a sense of humor.
Today, I will hit the pavement doubly quick.
Today, I will build my journey brick by brick.
Day by Day,
The Milestones of Life are Celebrated
Day by Day,
Good and Bad are both appreciated.

CHERRY FIREWORKS

This cherry bomb is about to blow!
It's about to explode!

I'm a bomb of divine possibilities.
I'm a bomb of divine treasures.
I'm a bomb of divine abilities.

This bomb is about to blow!
This bomb is about to explode!
I'm about to change!
I'm forming new patterns!
I'm starting a new page!

GREET THE DAY

Greeting each new day with prayer,
I achieve a state of non-fear.
Wearing my heart on my sleeve,
I go through each day with such ease.

STRIVE ON

Strive for your inner child;
Strive to keep your reaction mild.
Strive for your own well-being.
Strive for your right to practice the art of achieving; Strive
for your faith to improve yourself.
Strive for your life when you have no one else.
Strive to be strong;
Strive to move on,
Till your inner battle is won!
Strive on!

MOVING UP

Moving upward
Leaving the past behind
Moving forward
Listening to my inner child

JUST DREAM

Dream for your soul.
Dream of a world that is whole.
Dream of touching the sky.
Dream of big things.
And keep your dream alive!

THE AWAKENING FORCE
(RHAPSODY)

I know to go the extra mile.
I know to be kinder.
I know to expand my mindset with growth.
I know my inner work thrives with more effort.

I know I'm learning to trust the process.
I know to be more merciful.
I know my life is getting better and better.
I know good things will come easily.

I know every day is a treasure.
I know I am free to choose.
I know powerful changes are happening.

I welcome the swarming butterflies,
For I know I am loved!

YES

I am a YES!
Insatiable for success,
A warm sense of harmony infuses my chest
As I repeat these words in my heart:
HAPPINESS AND SUCCESS,
HAPPINESS AND SUCCESS,
HAPPINESS AND SUCCESS!

LEADING CHANGE

I toil in quietude,
Individuality speaking.
I focus on becoming more,
Investing in self,
Transforming from inside out.
For doing the Creator's will raises me up.

PUSH FORWARD

As I push forward,
The chips may fall where they may,
But every action has a price you must pay.
Praying to push forward each and every single day,
I strive to live right in every way.
For it's clear as a crystal ball:
A deer that blazes through traffic sees it all.
Blinded by bright lights,
It fights for its dear life!
But it shall hold its own,
Crossing wild barriers of the unknown
Even against oncoming traffic.
The deer's fearless eyes get graphic.
Conscious of the principles of nature,
It senses the intersecting forces of danger,

But still moves forward.

Determined to leap over obstacles,
The deer listens to its spirit,
Which drives it to cross to the other side.
Still compelled to try

In the face of failing
To reach greener pastures,
As the Supernatural is its master,
It kicks the ground for good luck,
Risks its unborn fawn's fate,
And leaps across the road like a spring buck.

Crashing to its knees like James Dean,
It soon recovers from the halls of the Unseen,
For a little step forward is a big step taken.
So find your own gift to awaken,
AND PUSH FORWARD!

BECOMING ONE WITH THE GOD SOURCE

Become one with love.
Discover the vast power within you.
So true.

As an exceptional being,
That highest good flows through you.
So true.

Trust in its power.
There's so much in store for you.
So true.

ESSENTIAL MOTION

Find the grace to change.
CHANGE!
Keep the dream alive for the new age.
CHANGE!
Have the courage to make a difference.
CHANGE!
Harbor true faith in deliverance!

OM!

SOPRANO HALLS

I travel to the ocean
To hear the pleas of my soul.
Brushing aside the colorless voices that clamor,
I keep believing in my ability to grow!

PRESENTLY THINKING

As I stay afloat in silence,
Lingering fear crystallizes into darkness.
For I win on courage,
I win on faith,
I stand undisturbed,
BEING ONE WITH THE WAVES.
For there is a presence one can call
A presence of ample supply,
A presence that loves all,
A presence of higher mind.
A presence that is always on time!

CHOOSE WISELY

As you're choosing your thoughts,
You're choosing your life.
So be kind while striving
for all you desire,
So you gain a worthwhile slice of life.

THIS IS REALITY

You must be wiser.
You must be stronger.
You must think smarter.
You must be calmer.
You must work harder.
You must be happier.
You must live lighter.
You must run the race farther.
You must wake up; it's now or never!
For we were born of divine love!

BREATHE IN

It's time to breathe in the saliferous green sea.
Inhale the aroma as you feel the rugged bark of the tree.
Just simply tune in,
And sense the momentum building within.
Don't wait another minute.
Step into your truth with good intention,
And fully live it!

INFINITE HUES

Where can you turn
When dusky days, they blind you,
And the color of joy fades to blue?

Where can you turn but inward,
To attune with your real self
And live in your truth?

To be continued …

BURSTING OUT

With divine spirit behind,
I beat my drum as a Buddha warrior.
As a one-of-a-kind,
I thrive from within to exceed ever further.
Choosing a new frame of mind.
I stay open to learning more.

Sending ciphers in the wind
While choosing to explore more,
I burst out a smile every chance that I get.
Though as we know,
The game's not over yet.

AMPLIFY

Amplify the life you know you deserve. Amplify
A certain amount of nerves. Amplify
Your soul and thrive on high vibes. Amplify
Your full potential all of the time.
Amplify,
For you're a gift to creation.

CHAPTER 6
INDIGO PETALS

I rise like the sun,
Stepping into my purpose.
As my soul grows in age,
My true self becomes one!

EYE OF THE STORM

You are the wind that blows.
Take charge of your reactions.
For you are the eye of the storm,
Undisturbed when transformed.

UPGRADE YOUR REALITY

Squelch the shadows with your light.
Snatch the deer by the horns.
Shift to a higher existence,
For you were divinely made right!

WHAT IS TRUE

Over the clouds, I'm soaring,
Flowing with the wind as it waltzes,
As blue lava irradiates the universe,
And angels guide my divine path,
Knowing my inner calling is true!

ASTRALLY HIGH

Thoughts can manifest anything, so
I cultivate a positive mentality,
Making the best of all I encounter,
Building a bridge of wisdom over murky, muddy waters.
For I am an astral warrior
Blazing
Astrally
High.

FINDING PEACE

In strange lands
Wandering onward,
My footsteps fade among the sand.
As the light of hope takes my hand,
Life becomes possible again.
For I resurrected a greater plan
By being who I truly AM!

THE DIVINE'S PERFECT REFLECTION

The winning purpose of my soul vibrates,
Actualizing winning conditions in my life.

With grace,

I glow with absolute perfection,
Guided by an everlasting presence.

I AM the Divine's perfect reflection!

CHANGE WITHIN

Change within,
For your mind changes,
Energy changes,
The world changes,
When WE
Change within!

COURAGEOUS LION

A master of true self-awareness,
I am a queen
with a thankful attitude.
If I can start a new chapter
So can the champion in you!

TRUST THE DIVINE

There is divine guidance
Knocking on your door every day.
Trust in the process
And allow yourself to slip
Along the way.
For the well of love is near,
and a rainbow of love is great.
How you play with life
Determines your divine fate!

METAMORPHOSIS

I am blessed beyond my deepest dreams.
I am conscious of my soul's purpose.
Moving through the gateway to more enriching experiences,
I enjoy everything I do.
Contributing to humanity in a meaningful way,
I accept myself as I am.
I am blessed beyond measure.
What a blessing to be simply living!

IT'S YOUR CHOICE

Life is a choice.
Electrify your life
like it's the Fourth of July.
DO SOMETHING POSITIVE!
Let go of worry;
Manifest like a butterfly.
The universe will do the rest.
For doing what is good for your life
Is the ultimate quest.

RED RIVER TRAILS

With just one step ahead,
I navigate through turbulence
As the pursuit of divine calling brings purpose.
My sailing spawns a succession of waves.
Knowing that love will always save the day,
I forge through deep waters,
Unraveling the minds of the wise,
Awakening to the sound of progression.
For it is time to arise!

FLY WITH THE WIND

I fly with the wind,
Going within,
Being my dearest friend.
I'll stick through it all till the end.

Even if I fail,
I'll start again till I win,
Winning a good life,
Doing the right thing,
Awakening within.

CHAPTER 7
VIOLET CROWN

Beheld by the Eternal light,
I embrace the glory of Eternal light
And honor my soul!

SAILING ON

Go with the flow;
Allow inner balance to guide your soul.
As you ride the river,
Keep a positive attitude forever.
As you glide over the waves,
Let love feel good each and every day.

I IGNITE MY SPIRIT

If you only knew that I'm

Attentive as stone,
Sweet as the tears of the Nile.
I am a sacred fire on my own,
Being eternally willing to go the extra mile.
Drumming around a circle of wow,
I imaginatively seek a divine fit.
Plowing along here and now,
I aspire to fly to where the Creator sits.
And as I rise from the ashes
And from the heart of sound,
I flow to harmonic frequencies floating by,
Where trauma water can be found
Fading into the sky.

INFINITE BUTTERFLY

Originality is yours.
Unstoppable, you are.
Your mentality is eminently perfect,
For you are vibrating sounds from the cosmos,
Playing the starry notes of life.

FLYING LIVELY

Flying into peacefulness,
I fly into activeness.
Flying into clarity,
I fly into optimistic energy.
For I fly constantly,
Flapping my wings with certainty!

BUILDING THE BEDROCK

With burning devotion,
I'm forging a rewarding life.
With the power to act,
I'm anchored by desire,
Transforming into light!

SACRED EYES

I see myself as loving.
I see myself as forgiving.
I see myself becoming alive.
I see myself learning to thrive.
I see myself with new beginnings.
I see myself forever surrendering,
Seeing myself
As a child of divine infinity.

AWAKE

As an infinite being,
My life flows so clearly.
As I walk in the light,
I am aware of my being.

CELLS OF WISDOM

Through every moment you are alive,
Shine like energy from the divine.
While oozing streams of positive vibes,
Align with spirit as you shine!
For you must take each day to new heights,
Bringing magic into your light!

ASCENDING

I rise higher,
Rising
Higher.
Across the purple skies,
I fly higher
And higher
Over the sunrise till I'm wise.
And there,
Along the Milky Way,
My wishes shine over a starlit bay.
And there,
I count ripples of ether from afar,
Where waves climax into shooting stars.
Then, seeing the cosmic ocean bed glistening,
I realize the divine queen sings within me!

ONE

Be the One Life
In this One World.
Be a force of One Love
United with the One Mind,
The universal God from below and above.

CALLIGRAPHIC INNER DIVINE

As each cloud sails across the sky,
You should look up high.
For clearly, I
Am leading you to the summit of eternity.
So stretch your heart space to the stars
And know God's love is bigger than Mars.
But as you face danger like a samurai warrior,
Honor your galactic cells
By sketching out your future fate.
For it's never too late!

BE HAPPY

Be happy to be alive!
Be happy to stumble and survive!
Be happy to have a divine soul!
Be happy to be young and old!

A RISING STAR

Be proud you made it this far,
For there's nothing greater or better
Than realizing you
Are a shining star.

I WAKE UP

I rise like the sun,
Stepping into my purpose.
As my soul grows in age,
My true self becomes one!

www.ingramcontent.com/pod-product-compliance
Lightning Source LLC
Chambersburg PA
CBHW031549040426
42452CB00006B/249